FLIP FLOP FRENCH

Ages 3-5: Level 1
A Learning Workbook

by
Yvonne Manette Batot
Señora Gose

Special thanks to:
Frances Jasik Batot
Brian A. Crawford
Righteous Rain Productions

Other titles by Flip n Flop Learning LLC:

Spanish Fun Activity Calendar
Flip Flop Spanish: Ages 3-5: Level 1
Flip Flop Spanish: Ages 3-5: Level 2
Flip Flop Spanish Flash Cards: Verde
Al revés inglés: nivel 1: edades 3 hasta 5

ISBN 978-1-60402-967-3

Published in the United States of America

by Flip n Flop Learning LLC
2009 Vinewood Drive
Bryan, TX 77802

www.flipfloplearning.com

You *can* teach your child French!

Teaching your child is a wonderful experience for all parties involved. It is our hope that this workbook will allow you to learn and teach French, following along easily, working page by page, lesson by lesson, to completion. With a little dedication and motivation, your child will have a working knowledge of French by the end of the fourteen lessons.

Lesson Time: Each lesson should last approximately one week. The Lesson Page is designed for the parent. First, the parent should read the lesson (aloud or silently), listen to the corresponding CD track, and then lead the child through the following three or four activities. Always begin by going over the vocabulary several times with your student before attempting the activities. Listening to the CD in the car is also a great way to introduce your student to each lesson. There's nothing like a "captive audience!"

Activity Time: Each daily lesson activity (labeled Un through Quatre) should take between ten and fifteen minutes (sometimes only five) to complete. If your child gets frustrated, it is best to put the workbook aside and come back to that page later in the day or perhaps even the next day. The most important aspect is for your child to be exposed to French a little each day.

Consistency: For increased retention, students should do one activity per weekday, listen to the CD track, or even review a completed activity. If you miss a day, do not fret. Lessons sometime have fewer activities to allow for weeks when "life happens." All in all, your child should be able to work through and master the entire book in fifteen weeks' time: one lesson per week, with an added week for translation pages and review.

How to use this book:

This parent, teacher, and child-friendly workbook is designed specifically so that you get the most out of your French experience. Every other page is inverted (upside-down, or flip-flopped) to give your student several benefits.

The "flip-flop" set-up keeps your child from ever having to reach across a spiral to write or draw, enables him to focus on one page at a time, and also guarantees that he will re-visit his previously completed activities as he turns the pages, working back through the second half of the book.

As your child uses the book, simply fold the book back so that only one page is facing up. When you complete lesson seven, turn the book upside down, and work back toward the front, continuing to fold each page back. You and your student will encounter review items as well as new lessons on the "return journey."

You will notice icons in the top corners of each page that quickly instruct your child as to the nature of the lesson on that page.

 = **LOOK and LISTEN.** This page includes new vocabulary words and instruction for the lessons ahead. No written work is required on these pages.

 = **WRITE-ON.** This page requires coloring, drawing, writing, acting, or other written activities.

Included in this curriculum is a CD, recorded by Shawna Fox and produced by Righteous Rain Productions, to assist you and your child with proper pronunciation of each new word as well as provide your student with more speaking practice.

= **CD TRACK.** Each lesson number corresponds to a track on the CD.

For more information, as well as free e-mail tutoring advice, please contact Yvonne Manette Batot via e-mail:
yvonne@yvonnebatot.com

Table of Contents

Lesson I

New vocabulary:

French	**Sounds like**	**English**
merci	mehr-see	thank you
de rien	duh-ree-ehn	you're welcome
s'il vous plait	see-voo-play	please
bonjour	bohn-zhuhr	good day/hello
salut	sa-loo	hi

Pointers:

- In French, you often do not pronounce the last consonant in a word. Frequently the last consonant is barely heard.

  le chat (luh-sha) - the cat   la main (lah-mehn) - the hand   un (uhn) - one

- When the last letter of a word is an 'e' without an accent, it is silent, you only pronounce the preceding consonant. If the 'e' has an accent mark then pronounce the 'e'.

  la tête (lah-teht) - the head   le carré (luh-cah-ray) - square

- Unlike English, there is usually not any stress on individual syllables in French words.

Translation Page 2

Answer the following questions in French.

1. Comment t'appelles tu?

____

2. Comment ça va?

____

3. Est-ce que tu aimes les oranges?

____

4. Décrivez votre mère?

____

5. Décrivez votre père?

____

note: votre (voh-trah) is a polite way of saying your

Un

For each picture below, say and write the correct French etiquette word.

Translation Page I

Do you agree with the following statements?
Respond with **oui** or **non**.

1. J'aime les gros chiens. __________
2. Je n'aime pas les pommes. __________
3. Ma mère est grande. __________
4. Mon père est petit. __________

Pronounce each word below.

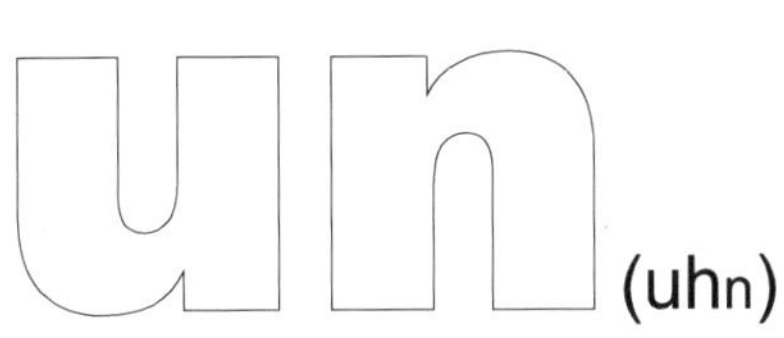

(uhn)

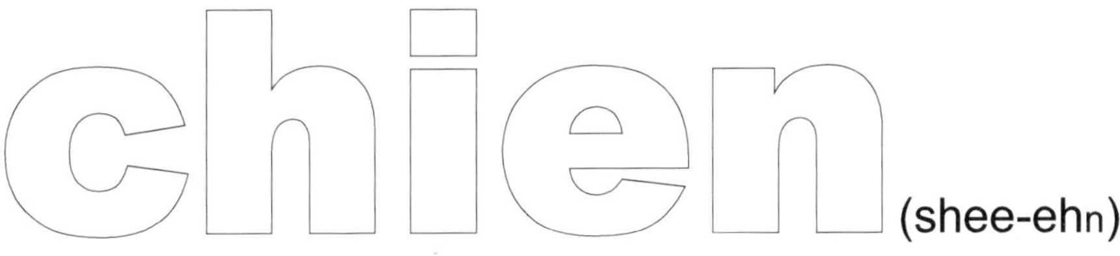

(shee-ehn)

(bay-bay)

(sha)

Now say each word again and cross out the letters that you do not pronounce.

Trois

Write a French weather phrase or word for each day this week
(the days are listed in French on the right.)

Monday ______________________________ lundi
(luhn-dee)

Tuesday ______________________________ mardi
(mahr-dee)

Wednesday ______________________________ mercredi
(mehr-kreh-dee)

Thursday ______________________________ jeudi
(zhuh-dee)

Friday ______________________________ vendredi
(vahn-dreh-dee)

Saturday ______________________________ samedi
(sam-dee)

Sunday ______________________________ dimanche
(dee-mahnsh)

Trois

Use your vocabulary! Follow these directions during the day today.
Then write the correct French word in the blank.

Your mom helps you and you say thank you:

____

A friend says hello, and you say: _______________________

You are asked if you would like more juice, so you say "please": _______________________

How many times did you say *merci* today? ☐

How many times did you say *bonjour* today? ☐

How many times did you say *s'il vous plait* today? ☐

Match each picture with the correct French word.

le torrent

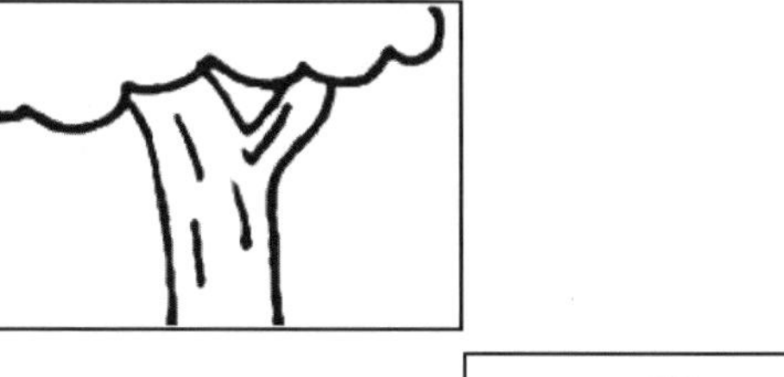

le vent

la pluie

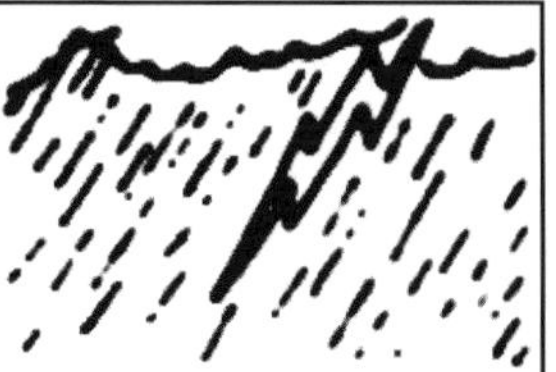

l'arbre

la neige

Lesson 2

New vocabulary:

French	Sounds like	English
comment ça va?	koh-moh-sa-va	how are you?
bien	bee-ehn	good/fine
comme-ci comme-ça	kohm-see-kohm-sah	so-so
mal	mal	bad
très	treh	very

Pointers:

- For older students, add the following phrases to this lesson as well:

je suis	zhuh-swee	I am
et tu?	ay-too	and you?

- Use the following pictures to teach your child the different emotions:

Un

Tell your Mom or Dad what each item is below,
then ask them to help you write the words in French.

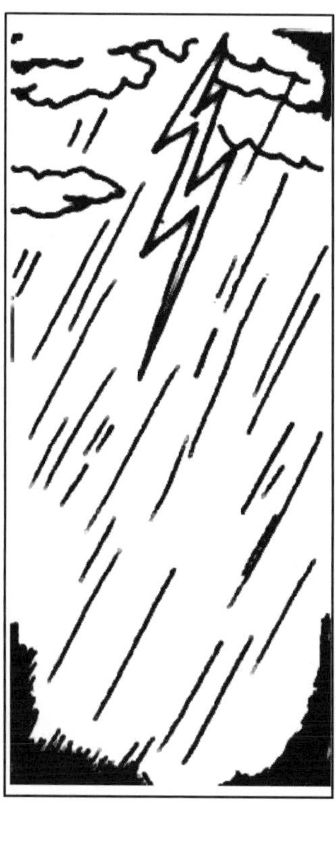

Un

Fill in each face according to the French word below it.
Be sure to say the word aloud three times as you draw.

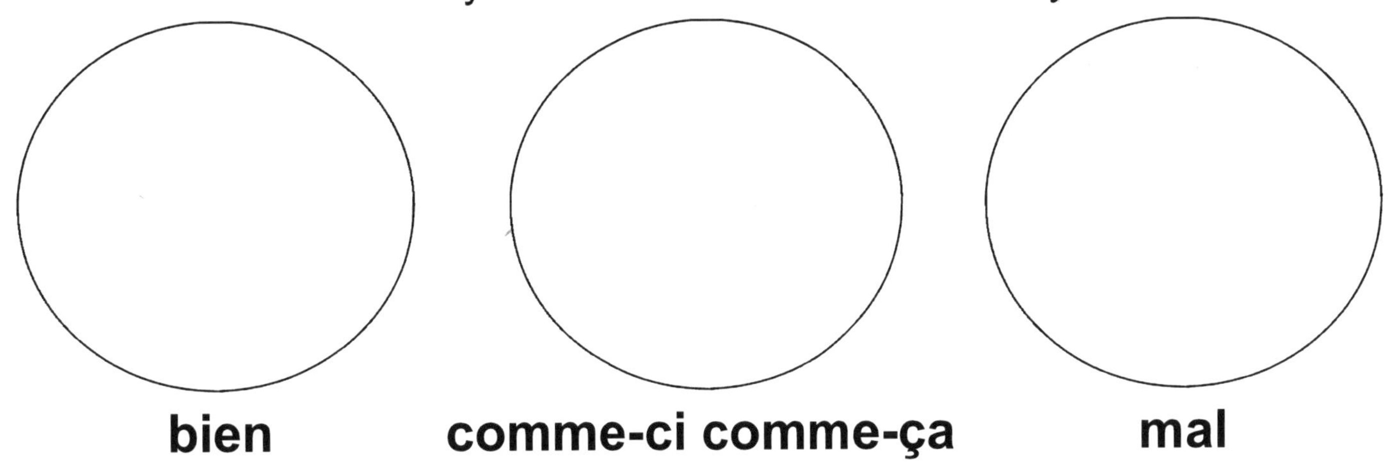

♬ ♬ Deux ♬ ♬

Use the tune "Skip to My Lou" to sing the words below. Point to the faces you drew as you sing. You can add thumbs-up and thumbs-down motions, too!

Comment ça va? Ça va bien.

Comment ça va? Ça va mal.

Comment ça va? Comme-ci comme-ça.

Comment ça va? Bien, Merci.

14

Lesson 14

New Vocabulary:

French	Sounds like	English
la pluie	lah-ploo-ee	the rain
le vent	luh-vehnt	the wind
le torrent	luh-tohr-rahn	the storm
la niege	lah-nehj	the snow
la fleur	lah-fluhr	the flower

Pointers:

- Use the newspaper forecast and pictures to practice weather words.

- This is your last lesson! Congratulations on completing your child's first French textbook. On the final page, you'll find some French phrases that you and your child should be able to understand, repeat, and then use.

- Continue to incorporate French in weekly lessons through flashcards, speaking, and library books. When your child is ready, look for Flip Flop French: Ages 3-5 Level 2! Also, be sure to fill out and send in the coupon at the back of the book to have a certificate mailed directly to your child.

Trois

Look at the faces below. Pretend they are speaking French! Ask each one: *Comment ça va?* What will they answer?

Ask three people today, *Comment ça va?* Show them how to answer in French using the hand motions for thumbs up, thumbs down, and so-so.

Quatre

Draw a line from each French word to its meaning.

mal	very
bien	so-so
comme-ci comme-ça	I am
je suis	good/fine
très	bad

Trois

Match each word with the correct picture.

le soleil

le chien

le nuage

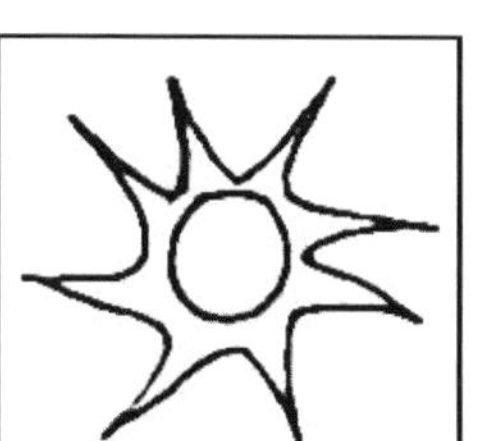

Quatre

While you're in the car, point out the words on the list and say them in French. See if you can find each word twice.

le chat	**le chien**
l'arbre	**la voiture** *lah-vwah-chuhr* **(the car)**
le nuage	**la fleur** *lah-fluhr* **(the flower)**
la rue	**l'oiseau**

Lesson 3

New vocabulary:

French	Sounds like	English
rouge	roozh	red
blanc	blahn	white
bleu	bluh	blue
un	uhn	one
deux	deuh	two
trois	twah	three
quatre	katr	four
cinq	sank	five
six	sees	six

Pointers:

- Your child should speak numbers as he sees them rather than count up to each one.
- You may also ask **Combien?** (kohm-bee-ehn**)** - How many? - for more practice with numbers.
- Colors can be found in abundance all around us. Have your child name them in French as he sees them throughout the day.

Add drawings of the words listed below to the landscape.
Say each word three times as you draw.

l'arbre	l'oiseau
le nuage	la rue

Now say what color you used for each item in French.

Un

Color the flags, rouge, blanc, and bleu for the top one and rouge and blanc for the second one. As you color, repeat the name of each color.

As you ride in the car today, see how many bleu, blanc, and rouge cars you see. Call out the names of the colors in French as you see them!

Un

Color the picture according to the guide below.

l'arbre = vert

le nuage = gris

le soleil = jaune

la mer (*lah-mehr* - the sea) = bleu

le ciel (*luh-see-ehl* - the sky) = bleu, rose, et orange

Deux

These numbers are out of order!
Point to each one and then say the number in French.
Then say them in order.

5 3 6 1 2 4

un deux trois quatre cinq six

13

New vocabulary:

French	Sounds like	English
l'arbre	lahrbr	the tree
le soleil	luh-soh-lay	the sun
le nuage	luh-noo-ahzh	the cloud
la rue	lah-roo	the street

Pointers:

- This week, look out the window or take a walk to introduce the new words. Have your child count the clouds in the sky or the trees in your yard to review numbers, and indicate whether they are big or small to review adjectives.
- **New verb to use with this lesson:** **il y a** (eel-ee-ah) means "there is" and "there are".

  Il y a deux nuages. = There are two clouds.

  Il n'y a pas d'arbres. = There are not any trees. (There are no trees.)

Trois

Count each item aloud (in French!) and write the number in the box.
For extra practice, write out the number in French on the line provided.

Trois

Draw a line from each French word to the correct picture:

les bottes

la veste

la chemise

Quatre

Your Mom or Dad will read a question to you. Go get each item out of your closet or drawers. Then, as the words are repeated, put each item back where you found it.

Où est ta veste?
(oo-eh-ta-vehst)
Where is your jacket?

Où est ta chemise?
(oo-eh-ta-sheh-meez)
Where is your shirt?

Où sont tes chausseurs?
(oo-sohn-tay-shoh-suhr)
Where are your shoes?

Où sont ton pantalon?
(oo-eh-tohn-pan-ta-lohn)
Where are your pants?

 4

Lesson 4

New vocabulary:

French	Sounds like	English
violet	vee-oh-leh	purple
brun(marron)	bruhn(ma-rohn)	brown
vert	vehr	green
jaune	zhohn	yellow
rose	rohz	pink
noir	nuahr	black
sept	seht	seven
huit	weet	eight
neuf	neuhf	nine
dix	dees	ten

Pointers:

- Remember, being able to count to ten in French does not signify the mastery of numbers, just as knowing the ABC song does not mean a child can recognize letters. Children should be able give the names of numbers on sight.

- Counting backwards from ten in French during the day during various activities will also strengthen a child's connection with the language.

Deux

Draw clothes on the people. Cross off each word as you design the clothes.
Be sure to say the name of each piece of clothing in French as you draw and color it.

les chausseurs	**la chemise**	**le pantalon**
la robe (dress) (lah-rohb)	**les bottes**	**le chapeau (hat)** (luh-shah-poh)

Un

Color the picture!
Write the color names (in French!) you used on each line.

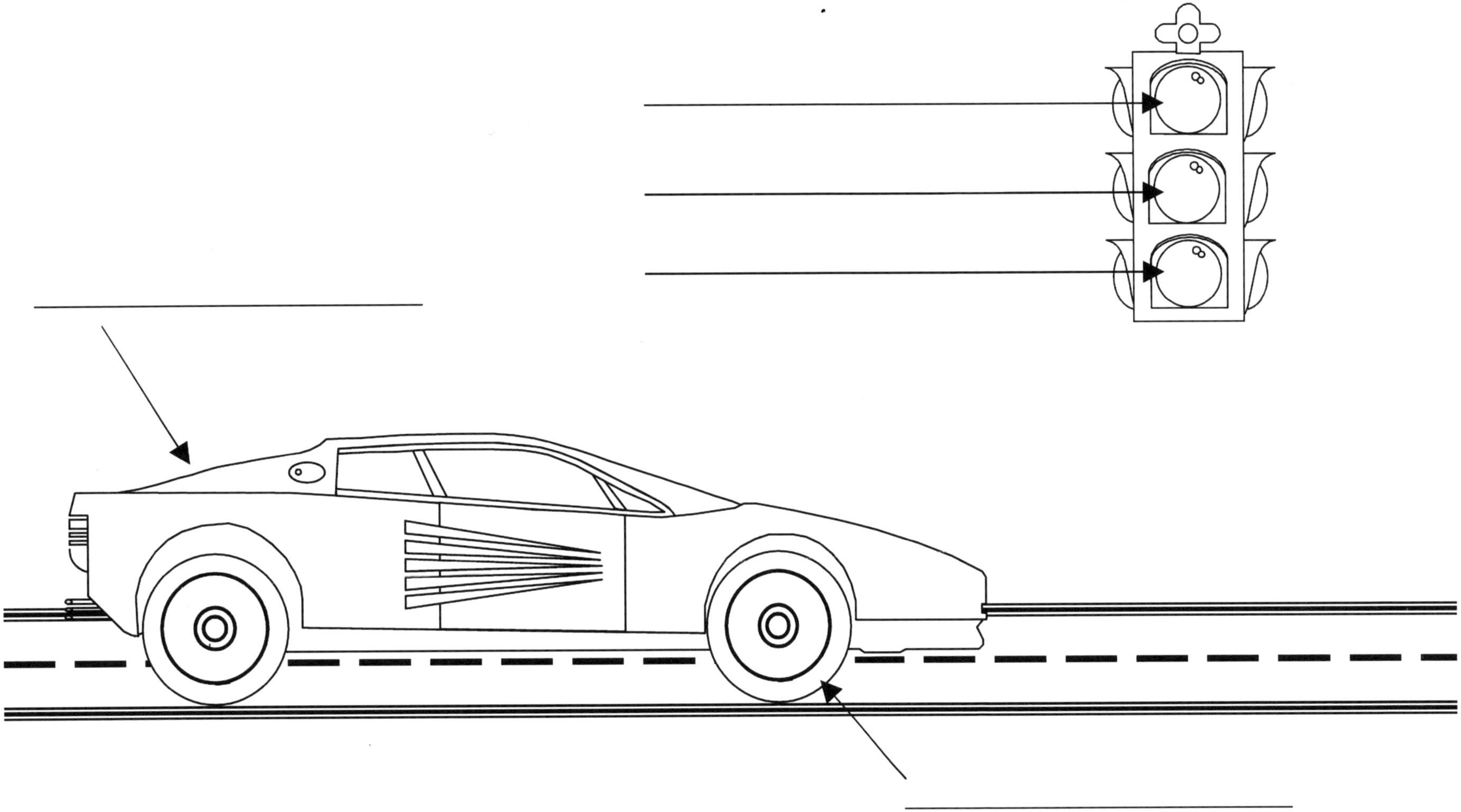

Un

Color the clothing while repeating the words below each picture.

la veste bleue

le pantalon brun

la chemise jaune

Match each French word with the corresponding number.

1	neuf
7	deux
5	sept
4	un
9	dix
2	cinq
10	quatre

Lesson 12

(((12

New vocabulary:

French	Sounds like	English
la chemise	lah-sheh-meez	the shirt
le pantalon	luh-pan-ta-lahn	the pants
les chaussures	lay-shoh-suhr	the shoes
la veste	lah-vehst	the jacket
le pullover	luh-puhl-oh-vehr	the sweater
les bottes	lay-baht	the boots

Pointers:

- When introducing this lesson, gather together the clothing named above in much larger sizes than your child wears (your own will do nicely). As you name the items together, have your child put them on while saying the French word three times for each piece.

- Some verbs to use with this section:

Je porte	(zhuh-pohrt)	I'm wearing
J'ai	(zhay)	I have

Trois

Draw the items in each box. Be sure to use the correct color!
When you finish, check your work and count the items again in French!
*French adjectives often follow the noun rather than precede it.

six *circles* **rouges**

deux *fish* **noirs**

quatre *potatoes* **brunes**

sept *triangles* **violets**

Trois

Draw a line from the English word to the correct French translation.

the arm	la tête
the head	la main
the foot	les doigts
the fingers	le pied
the hand	le bras

Quatre

Have your mom or dad help you fill in the blanks:

1. I clap my ________________________.
2. I stomp my ________________________.
3. I shake my ________________________.
4. I wiggle my ________________________.

Lesson 5

French	Sounds like	English
j'aime	zhehm	I like
je n'aime pas	zhuh-nehm-pa	I don't like
est-ce que tu aimes?	ehss-kuh-too-ehm	do you like?
et	ay	and
mon favori	mohn-fa-voh-ree	my favorite

Pointers:

- To compose a question in French, simply put 'Est-ce que' (ehss-kuh) in front of the subject and noun.

  Est-ce que tu aimes les poissons (pwah-sohn)? = Do you like the fish?

- The adjective often *follows* the noun in French. Therefore, "the brown dog" would be "le chien brun," and "my favorite toy" is "mon jouet favori." (mohn-zhoo-ay-fa-voh-ree)

- Pronunciation tip - When an 'h' is at the beginning of a word it is not usually pronounced.

  l'hotel (loh-tehl) - the hotel

Deux

Use the pictures and color or circle **only** the body part listed under each box.

les jambes

la tête

les pieds

Now point to other body parts you see and name them.

Un

Color the top two boxes with colors you LIKE.
Then tell your mom and dad: **J'aime (your color).**

J'aime ____________________

et _____________________________.

Now fill in the bottom box with a color you don't like.

Je n'aime pas ____________________ .

Point to each box and ask your parents:

Est-ce que tu aimes?

They should answer **oui** (wee) - yes; or **non** (nohn) - no.

Un

Color the man according to the list on the right.
Say each body part word
three times as you color it.

les bras = rouge

les jambes = violet

les mains = rose

les pieds = noir

la tête = rose

Do you remember the name of

the animal on his plate?

Deux

For each picture below, circle the answer **J'aime** or **Je n'aime pas**, and then complete the sentence about each item.

J'aime Je n'aime pas

...la pomme (lah-puhm).

J'aime Je n'aime pas

...le pain (luh-pehn).

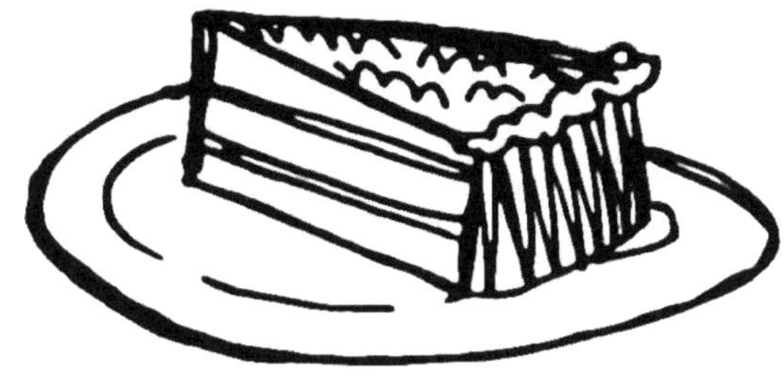

J'aime Je n'aime pas

...le gâteau (luh-ga-toh).

J'aime Je n'aime pas

...l'orange (lohr-ahnzh).

Lesson II

11

New vocabulary:

French	Sounds like	English
la tête	lah-teht	the head
la main	lah-mehn	the hand
les doigts	lay-dwaht	the fingers
le bras	luh-bra	the arm
la jambe	lah-zhahmb	the leg
le pied	luh-pee-ay	the foot

Pointers:

- When introducing this lesson, simply wave the indicated body part and say the word three times. Have your child do the same thing. You can add commands as well, with hints embedded in the commands:
    - Clap your mains.
    - Stomp your pieds.
    - Shake your tête.
    - Wave your bras.
    - Wiggle your doigts.

Trois

Fill in each box by drawing a picture of your favorite item from each category. Then ask your mom or dad to write the word on the blank. Finally, repeat each sentence aloud.

______________ est mon couleur (*color*; koo-luhr) favori.

______________ est mon jouet (*toy*; zhoo-ay) favori.

______________ est ma livre (*book;* leevr) favori.

______________ est mon animal (*animal*; a-nee-mal) favori.

Trois

Use the chart below to describe people you know.
First fill in the names of your family and friends.
Then circle the word that describes each person best.

Name	Décrivez
	vieux jeune
	drôle serieux
	content triste
	grand petit

Lesson 6

New vocabulary:

French	Sounds like	English
gros(se)	groh(grohss)	fat
maigre	may-gruh	thin
grand(e)	grahnd(grahnd)	big/tall
petit(e)	peh-tee(peh-teet)	small/short
sale	sal	dirty
propre	prahpr	clean
décrivez	day-kree-vay	describe

Pointers:

- There are three words for "the" in French. Use the chart below to help your child express "the" correctly as he describes items around him.

	singular	plural
masculine	le	les
feminine	la	les

- For words that start with vowels (*a,e,i,o,u*) or *h* and *y*, use l' instead of le or la.

l'éléphant (lay-lay-fahnt) = the elephant   l'aeroport (lehr-oh-pohr) = the airport

Deux

Match the opposites below.

vieux

propre

content

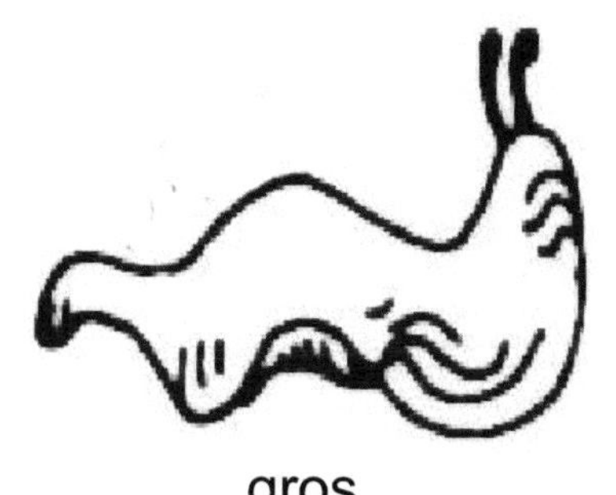

gros

petit

maigre

triste

sale

jeune

grand

Un

The best way to learn new adjectives is to act them out!
Play a game of charades or Simon Says with your parents,
repeating each adjective three times as you act it out.

Deux

Match the opposites below by drawing lines between them.
Then act the words out again as you say each one.

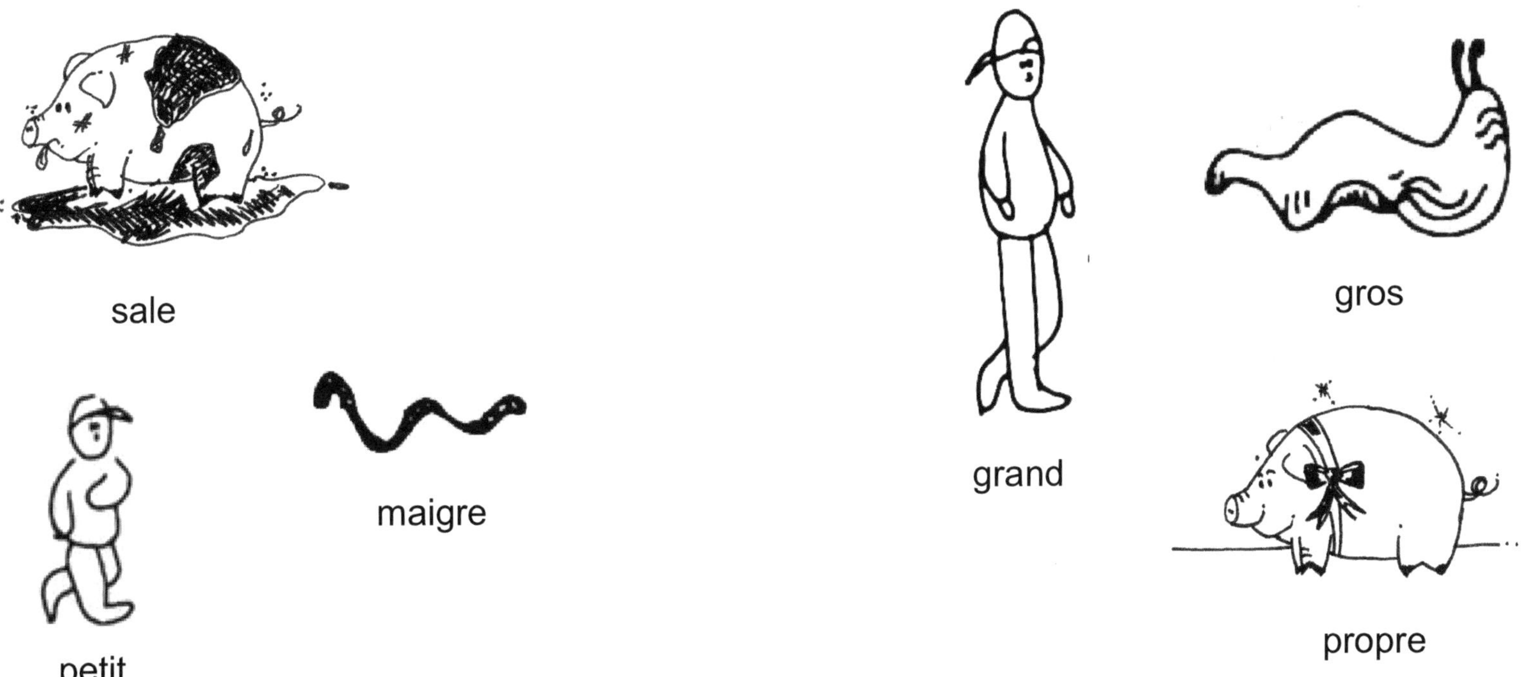

Un

Add to the people in each box to make them match the sentence below.

Jacques est gros.

Marie est intelligente et contente.

Nicole et Marc sont jeunes et drôles.

Trois

Look at the pictures below. Ask each question and fill in the blanks with the correct French adjectives.

Décrivez l'homme?
L'homme est ______________.

Décrivez le train?
Le train est _____________.

Décrivez la fille?
La fille est ______________.

Décrivez le chien?
Le chien est _____________.

Lesson 10

10

New vocabulary:

French	Sounds like	English
jeune	zhuhn	young
drôle	drohl	funny
sérieux(sérieuse)	sehr-ee-uh(sehr-ee-uhz)	serious
intelligent(e)	ihn-tehl-ee-zhohn	smart
triste	treest	sad
content(e)	kahn-tahn(kahn-tahnt)	happy

Pointers:

- This week your child will be looking at people in his family and describing them. Help your child to review all the adjectives, including numbers and colors they have learned up to now. This workbook does not cover family member names (see ***Flip Flop French Level 2***), but you may begin to use the following words to help your child describe people:

ma mère (mah-mehr) = my mother

mon père (mohn-pehr) = my father

Quatre

Use a new phrase: Je vois (zhuh-vwah) to say "I see".

Make sentences today by following the examples and patterns below. Please note that some adjectives come before the noun in French like petit/grand; gros/maigre.

Je vois le gros train.

Je vois la grande femme.

Je vois les petits garçons.

Je vois les camions (*trucks*; ka-mee-ohn) ________________.
(color or other adjective)

Je vois ______ ____________ ______________.
(le, la, or les) (noun: English or French) (adjective)

Trois

Fill in the chart with the names of food from your pantry. You can draw the food or ask your mom or dad to help you write the words.

J'AIME	JE N'AIME PAS

Quatre

Fill in the blanks with **J'AIME** or **JE N'AIME PAS**.

1. ______________________ les vieilles pommes.
2. ______________________ les bons (*bohn*-good) repas.
3. ______________________ les poires noires.
4. ______________________ les oranges brunes.

Lesson 7

New vocabulary:

French	Sounds like	English
le chien	luh-shee-ehn	the dog
le chat	luh-sha	the cat
l'ours	loors	the bear
le poisson	luh-pwah-sohn	the fish
l'oiseau	lwah-zoh	the bird

Pointers:

- Continue to use le, la and les, as well as the new adjectives to describe animals. Most male animal words can be made female by adding an *e* to the end and sometimes an extra *n* or *t*. For more advanced students, use this lesson to practice making adjectives agree with the noun:

The black dog.	=	Le chien noir.
The black female dog.	=	La chienne noire.

- Also use the new adjectives to describe yourself, using: Je suis (zhuh-swee) = I am

For males: Je suis grand. For females: Je suis grande.

Un

Connect the French word with the correct fruit by drawing a line.

la pomme

la poire

l'orange

Deux

At the grocery store, try to name the fruit you know in French.
Then speak the color after it:

La pomme rouge. = The red apple.
La poire verte. = The green pear.

Un

Color the animals below. Say the phrases below each picture three times as you color.

le chat brun

le gros chien

le grand oiseau

Lesson 9

9

New vocabulary:

French	Sounds like	English
la pomme	lah-puhm	the apple
l'orange	lohr-ahnzh	the orange
la poire	lah-pwahr	the pear
le fruit	luh-froo-ee	the fruit
le repas	luh-reh-pa	the meal
vieux(vielle)	vee-uh(vee-ay)	old
nuef(nueve)	neuhf(neuhv)	new

Pointers:

- Use your French in the grocery store or at the table with real items this week to help your child speak his new language in real-world situations! After nine weeks of practice, you both should be able to make original sentences now. Try and ask questions in French throughout the day, using the words below.

Est-ce que tu veux...?	ehss-kuh-too-vuh	Do you want…?
Quel?	kehl	Which?
Combien?	kohm-bee-ehn	How many?

Deux

Match the French Words with the correct picture.

le chien

le chat

l'ours

le poisson

l'oiseau

Trois

Now you be the reporter! Fill in the chart below with names of people and how they are feeling today. Be careful to speak only French!

In the first box, write their name; in the second box, write how they are today; and in the last box, write an adjective that describes them. You can draw pictures too!

Comment t'appelles tu?	Comment ça va?	Décrivez

Trois

As you watch TV, play outside, or look at books today, count how many of these animals you see.
Call out their names in French when you see them, then write the numbers below!

☐ chiens

☐ chats

☐ poissons

☐ ours

☐ oiseaux

Un

Do you have dolls or toys that have names? Pretend they can speak French!
Ask them what their names are and have them answer in French!
Ask your mom or dad to help you write three names on the lines:

Comment t'appelles tu?
Je m'appelle ______________________________.

Comment t'appelles tu?
Je m'appelle ______________________________.

Comment t'appelles tu?
Je m'appelle ______________________________.

Deux

Pretend you are on TV, and a reporter (your mom or dad) is asking you questions in French. Answer the questions aloud. Remember to speak French! For extra practice, you can write down your answers.

Bonjour, Comment t'appelles tu? ____________________
Enchanté, Comment ça va? ____________________
Au revoir. ____________________

Mid-Point Tips:

Now is a good time to invest in a set of flashcards or make your own using magazine pictures or simple drawings. **Sample flashcards** are included in the supplement pages at the back of this book. Whether or not you know the words in French, let your student make sentences in "Frenlish," reinforcing the words he knows, and allowing him to put words in the correct order according to French grammar rules.

Here are some examples of the types of sentences you might hear and encourage:

J'aime le kite bleu.

Je n'aime pas le spinach vert.

Le house est grand et rouge.

Le chat est très nice.

Though there are many English words in his phrases, your child is recognizing and *using* the French words he already knows. As with many skills; the old adages apply: "Practice, practice, practice!" and, "If you don't use it, you lose it."

Enjoy your journey back toward the front of the book! It is helpful to stop and review past lessons and compliment your child on the previously completed work, no matter how many weeks have passed.

Lesson 8

8

New vocabulary:

French	**Sounds like**	**English**
Comment t'appelles tu?	koh-moh-ta-pehl-too	What's your name?
Je m'appelle	zhuh-ma-pehl	My name is
enchanté	ahn-shahn-tay	Nice to meet you.
l'ami(e)	la-mee	the friend
le jouet	luh-zhoo-ay	the toy

Pointers:

- The question *Comment t'appelles tu?* is the familiar version used mainly between children or teenagers. To make an acquaintance with an adult that requires more formality, you would use *Comment vous appellez-vous? (koh-moh-vooz-a-pehl-ay-voo)*

- To introduce someone to someone else, the phrase is **Il s'appelle (his name is), Elle s'appelle (her name is)**

- For students craving more vocabulary, you can add more ways to say goodbye:

au revoir	(oh-reh-vwar)	goodbye
à bientôt	(a-byehn-toh)	see you later
à demain	(a-deh-mehn)	see you tomorrow

Flip the book over to continue with Lesson Eight.

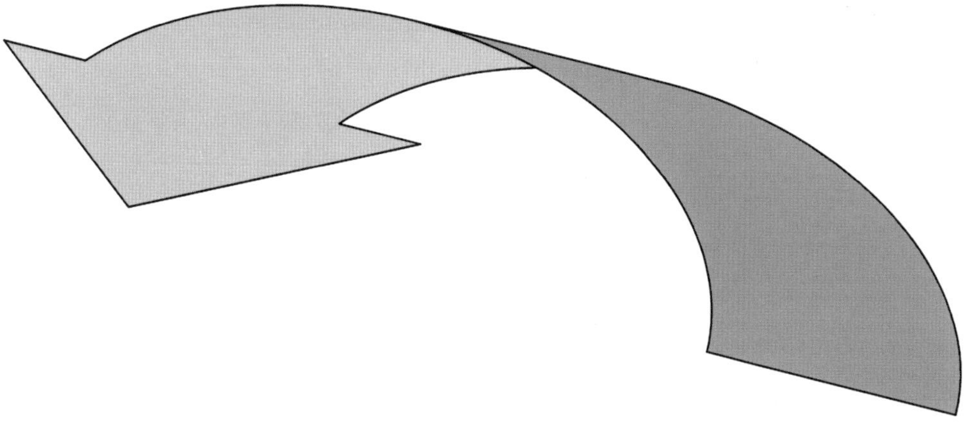

FLIP FLOP FRENCH continued...

Welcome to your return journey:

The *FLOP* of Flip Flop French.

Bon Voyage!
(Bohn voy-ahzh)
Have a good trip!

Continue with Lesson Eight on the “next” page.

SUPPLEMENTAL PAGES

GLOSSARY

English	French (*m/f - gender*)	Sounds like
airport	aeroport - *m*	ehr-oh-pohr
and	et	ay
and you?	et tu?	ay-too
animal	animal - *m*	a-nee-mal
apple	pomme - *f*	puhm
arm	bras - *m*	bra
baby	bébé - *m*	bay-bay
bad	mal	mal
bear	ours - *m*	oors
big	grand(e)	grahnd(grahnd)
bird	oiseau - *m*	wah-zoh
black	noir	nuahr
blue	bleu	bluh
book	livre - *m*	leevr

English	French	Sounds like
boots	bottes - *f*	baht
bread	pain - *m*	pehn
brown	brun(marron)	bruhn(ma-rohn)
cake	gâteau - *m*	ga-toh
car	voiture - *f*	vwah-chuhr
cat	chat - *m*	sha
clean	propre	prahpr
cloud	nuage - *m*	noo-ahzh
color	couleur - *f*	koo-luhr
describe	décrivez	day-kree-vay
dirty	sale	sal
do you like...?	est-ce que tu aimes?	ehss-kuh-too-ehm
do you want...?	est-ce que tu veux...?	ehss-kuh-too-vuh
dog	chien - *m*	shee-ehn
dress	robe - *f*	rohb
eight	huit	weet

English	French	Sounds like
elephant	éléphant - *m*	ay-lay-fahnt
fat	gros(se)	groh(grohss)
father	père - *m*	pehr
fingers	doigts - *m*	dwaht
fish	poisson - *m*	pwah-sohn
five	cinq	sank
flower	fleur - *f*	fluhr
food/meal	repas - *m*	rehpa
foot	pied - *m*	pee-ay
four	quatre	katr
friend	ami - *m*	a-mee
fruit	fruit - *m*	froo-ee
funny	drôle	drohl
good	bon(ne)	bohn(bun)
good/fine	bien	bee-ehn
good day/hello	bonjour	bohn-zhuhr

English	French	Sounds like
goodbye	au revoir	oh-reh-vwar
green	vert	vehr
hand	main - *f*	mehn
happy	content(e)	kahn-tahn(kahn-tahnt)
hat	chapeau - *m*	shah-poh
head	tête - *f*	teht
hi	salut	sa-loo
hotel	hotel - *m*	oh-tehl
how are you?	comment ça va?	koh-moh-sa-va
how many?	combien?	kohm-bee-ehn
I am	je suis	zhuh-swee
I am wearing	je porte	zhuh-pohrt
I don’t like	je n’aime pas	zhuh-nehm-pa
I have	j’ai	zhay
I like	j’aime	zhehm
I see	je vois	zhuh-vwah

English	French	Sounds like
jacket	veste - *f*	vehst
leg	jambe - *f*	zhahmb
my favorite	mon favori	mohn-fa-voh-ree
my name is	je m'appelle	zhuh-ma-pehl
new	neuf(nueve)	neuhf(neuhv)
nice to meet you	enchanté	ahn-shahn-tay
nine	neuf	neuhf
no	non	nohn
old	vieux(vielle)	vee-uh(vee-ay)
one	un	uhn
orange	orange - *f*	ohr-ahnzh
pants	pantalon - *m*	pan-ta-lahn
pear	poire - *f*	pwahr
pink	rose	rohz
please	s'il vous plait	see-voo-play
purple	violet	vee-oh-leh

English	French	Sounds like
question marker (is it that?)	est-ce que	ehss-kuh
rain	pluie - *f*	ploo-ee
red	rouge	roozh
sad	triste	treest
sea	mer - *f*	mehr
see you later	à bientôt	a-byehn-toh
see you tomorrow	à demain	a-deh-mehn
serious	sérieux(sérieuse)	sehr-ee-uh(sehr-ee-uhz)
seven	sept	seht
sky	ciel - *m*	see-ehl
shirt	chemise - *f*	sheh-meez
shoes	chaussures - *f*	shoh-suhr
six	six	sees
small/short	petit(e)	peh-tee(peh-teet)
smart	intelligent(e)	ihn-tehl-ee-zhohn
snow	niege - *f*	nehj

English	French	Sounds like
so-so	comme-ci comme-ça	kohm-see-kohm-sah
square	carré - *m*	cah-ray
storm	torrent - *m*	tohr-rahn
street	rue - *f*	roo
sun	soleil - *m*	soh-lay
sweater	pullover - *m*	puhl-oh-vehr
tall	grand(e)	grahnd(grahnd)
ten	dix	dees
thank you	merci	mehr-see
there is/there are	il y a	eel-ee-ah
thin	maigre	may-gruh
three	trois	twah
toy	jouet - *m*	zhoo-ay
tree	arbre - *m*	ahrbr
truck	camion - *m*	ka-mee-ohn
two	deux	deuh

English	French	Sounds like
very	trés	treh
what's your name?	comment t'appelles tu?	koh-moh-ta-pehl-too
what's your name?(polite)	Comment vous appellez-vous?	koh-moh-vooz-a-pehl-ay-voo
where	où	oo
which?	quel?	kehl
white	blanc	blahn
wind	vent - *m*	vehnt
yellow	jaune	zhohn
yes	oui	wee
young	jeune	zhuhn
you are welcome	de rien	duh-ree-ehn
your	ton/ta/tes	tohn/ta/tay
your (polite)	votre	voh-trah

gros

maigre

grand

petit

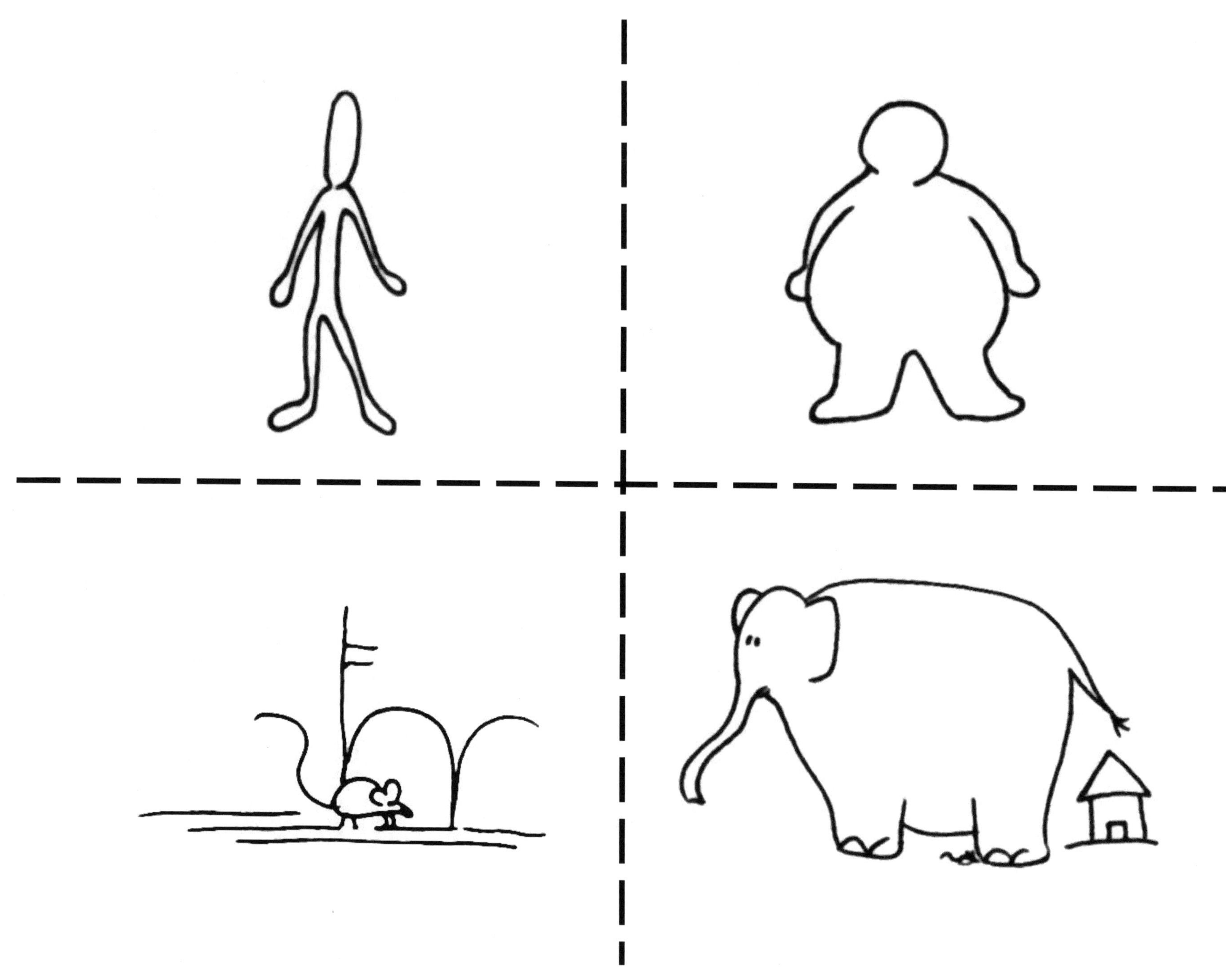

le chien

le chat

l'ours

le poisson

la main

la tête

les doigts

le bras

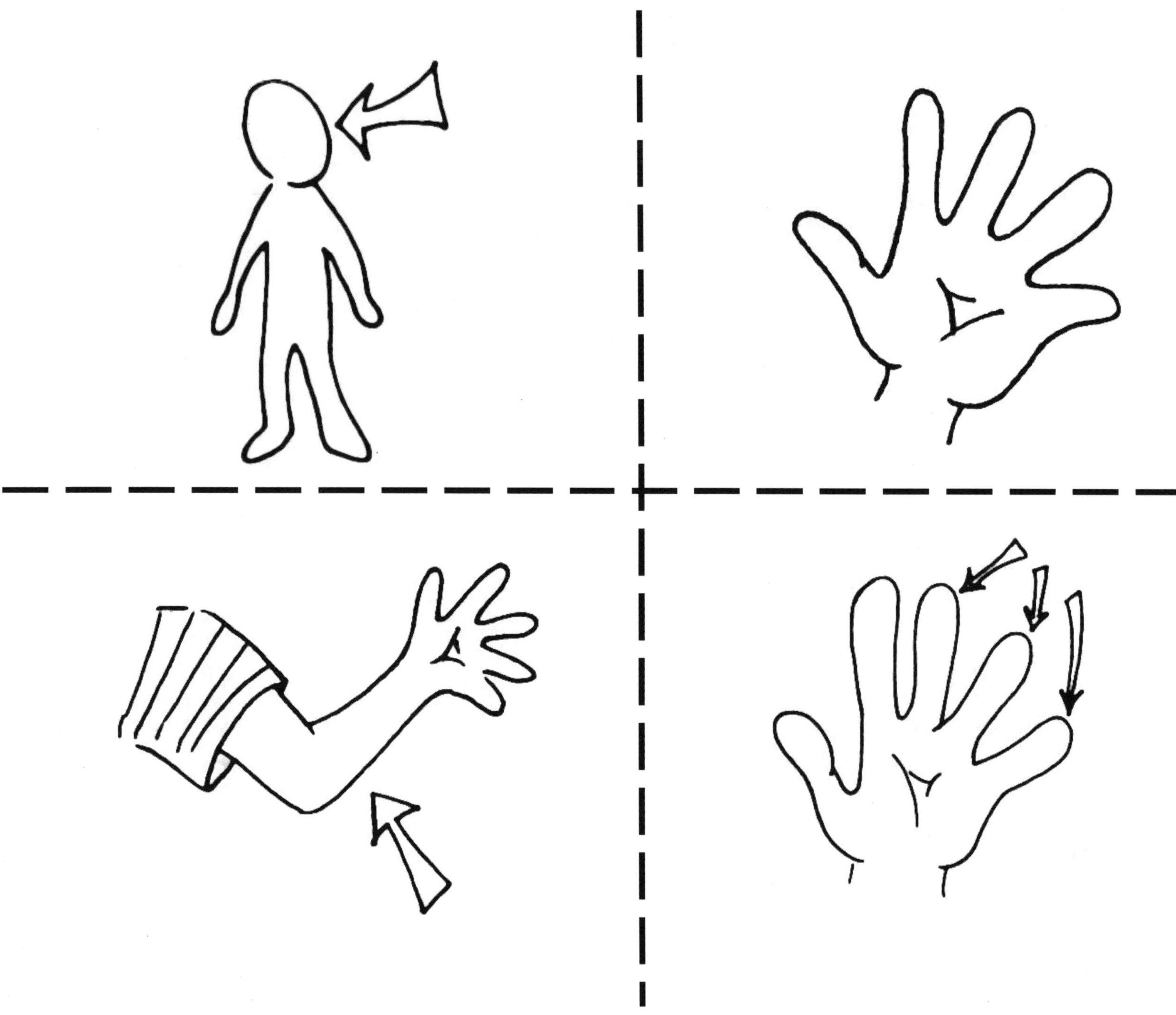

Thank you for purchasing Flip Flop French; Ages 3-5: Level 1. I hope the experience was fulfilling and rewarding for both you and your student. To continue with your child's French language education, please look for Flip Flop French; Ages 3-5: Level 2 at your favorite bookstore, or order online at:

www.flipflopfrench.com

Please check out our site for additional learning materials, FAQ's, and some free teaching tips!

Cut out and send in this coupon for a **FREE** personalized Certificate of Completion to be mailed directly to your child! Suitable for framing, it will be a visible reminder of his or her accomplishment!

Your Name ____

Child's Name _______________________________________

Mailing Address _____________________________________

City __________________ State ______ Zip _____________

Mail to: Flip Flop French, P.O. Box 6126, Bryan, TX 77805

Information will never be sold, transferred or distributed to a third party at any time, for any reason.